COPING

SEXUAL HARASSMENT

ROSE MCCARTHY

ROSEN PUBLISHING

Published in 2023 by The Rosen Publishing Group, Inc.
2544 Clinton St, Buffalo, NY 14224

First Edition

Designer: Rachel Rising
Editor: Corona Brezina

Portions of this work were originally authored by IV Thurston and published as *Coping with Sexual Harassment*. All new material in this edition authored by Rose McCarthy.

Cataloging-in-Publication Data

Names: McCarthy, Rose
Title: Sexual harassment / Rose McCarthy.
Description: New York : Rosen, 2023. | Series: Coping| Includes index and glossary.
Identifiers: ISBN 9781499473742 (pbk) | ISBN 9781499473759 (library bound) | ISBN 9781499473766 (ebook)
Subjects: LCSH: Sexual Harassment--Juvenile literature
Classification: LCC HQ1237 M33 2023 | DDC 305--dc23

Some of the images in this book illustrate individuals who are models. The depictions do not imply actual situations or events.

Manufactured in the United States of America

CPSIA Compliance Information: Batch #CSRYA23. For further information contact Rosen Publishing at 1-800-237-9932.

CONTENTS

CHAPTER 1

RECOGNIZING SEXUAL HARASSMENT

A driver yells a catcall at a girl as he drives past her in the street. A boss sends a sexually suggestive text message to an employee. A stranger touches another rider inappropriately in a crowded bus. A classmate makes a peer uncomfortable bragging about his sexual experiences. A colleague makes a homophobic comment during a work meeting. A high school student begins to stalk a classmate when she refuses his advances.

These are all examples of sexual harassment. According to a 2018 survey by the group Stop Street Harassment, 81 percent of women and 43 percent of men in the United States had experienced some form of sexual harassment and/or assault. The most common form was verbal sexual harassment, but 51 percent of women and 17 percent of men reported unwelcome touching or groping.

Legally, sexual harassment is defined as unwelcome sexual advances, requests for sexual favors, and other verbal or physical actions of a sexual nature. According to the Civil Rights Act of 1964, sexual harassment is a form of sex discrimination. This definition and the penalties for violations apply to workplaces. Students are likewise protected from sexual harassment by Title IX of the Education Amendments of 1972, which prohibits sex discrimination in schools and educational programs that receive federal funds. For situations outside the workplace and school, local and state laws generally apply. A harasser might be charged with an offense such as disorderly conduct or sexual battery. A few states have laws specifically addressing sexual harassment in public places.

Schools are required to post their sexual harassment policies publicly and have a Title IX coordinator in charge of preventing sex discrimination.

UNWELCOME ADVANCES

The key word in the aforementioned definition is "unwelcome." You are allowed to do anything you want within the law with someone if both parties consent. Courts have generally concluded that victims of sexual harassment do not have to show that they were not interested for harassment to occur. To think of it another way, assume that people do not want to talk to you, touch you, or do anything else in a sexual manner. That is normal. What is not normal is harassment. It is important to remember, at all times, that every victim of sexual harassment is exactly that: a victim.

If you have experienced unwelcome advances, do not be afraid to speak out. You have been wronged and did nothing to invite the other person's behavior, comments, or actions. Also, do not be afraid to speak out if you witness someone being sexually harassed. Ignoring harassment is not a useful strategy. Harassers rarely voluntarily stop harassing people. Sexual harassment is when someone makes you feel uncomfortable or upset because he or she did something unwanted to you and it included sexual overtones. Sexual harassment is also a form of bullying. Like all bullying, it is designed to hurt someone or make him or her afraid. Not only is the definition of sexual harassment broad, it can manifest itself in many ways. Here is a partial list of actions that definitely qualify as sexual harassment:

- Making sexual gestures
- Talking about someone in a lewd manner
- Making sexualized "jokes"

- Repeatedly asking someone out even after the person has said no
- Spreading rumors of a sexual nature—this can be done person to person, via text, or on social media
- Purposefully rubbing up against someone to touch his or her body
- Writing or drawing sexual graffiti about someone in a public place
- Touching, grabbing, or pinching someone in a sexual way or in his or her genital area(s)
- Sharing pornography with someone
- Saying sexualized things about someone or making offers to someone using a fake name or anonymously online
- Requesting "nudes" (naked photographs) or sending naked pictures of themselves
- Sending sexual messages of any form or posting sexual content on someone else's social media page(s)

Sexual harassment may be more likely to occur in a hostile work environment where inappropriate behavior is tolerated rather than penalized.

It is important to know that sexual harassment is not the same as sexual assault. While sexual harassment is not to be tolerated, sexual assault is someone physically acting on his or her desires when the other person does not want it. Sexual assault can be something as small as an unwanted kiss and as horrible as forced sexual intercourse or rape. Whether it is sexual harassment or assault, remember that it is never your fault that these things happened!

If someone is making you uncomfortable with inappropriate behavior, tell them firmly to stop—but only if you feel safe speaking up.

CLARENCE THOMAS VERSUS ANITA HILL

In 1991, President George H. W. Bush nominated federal judge Clarence Thomas to serve on the Supreme Court. During Thomas's confirmation hearings, a law professor named Anita Hill accused him of sexual harassment during the time that she had worked for him in the Office of Civil Rights of the U.S. Department of Education and the Equal Employment Opportunity Commission (EEOC) in the 1980s. She testified that Thomas had asked her out repeatedly despite her refusals and discussed graphic sexual topics in front of her. She was afraid to speak up at the time because she was afraid of losing her job. Thomas denied her claims.

Hill was questioned in a televised hearing by the Senate Judiciary Committee, made up of 14 white men. It was the first time a woman had gone public with an account of sexual harassment in such high-profile circumstances. The Senate eventually confirmed Thomas 52-48 in the closest Supreme Court confirmation vote since the 19th century. Anita Hill received death threats and accusations of lying in her testimony, but she never regretted speaking up.

About 20 million Americans watched the Clarence Thomas confirmation hearings, and women across the country realized that they were not alone in their experiences of sexual harassment.

INNOCENT FLIRTATION

Flirting is a gray area. The easiest way to know if something is flirtation or harassment is to answer this question: Do both people want this to happen, or is it only one person? Here are some examples that may help you understand the crucial difference between flirting and harassment.

- You and your boyfriend or girlfriend have been starting to get serious together. You joke about sending nudes to each other, and then when asked if you would send one, you say, "No way!" Instead of respecting your wishes, your partner continues to pressure you to do so. This is harassment.

- You wear a new outfit to school. A classmate tells you that it looks nice. That is not harassment. That is simply a compliment. If that person then tells you that it makes you look sexy or that your clothes make them want to do sexual things to you, that is harassment.

- A classmate asks you out on a date. You are not attracted to them and don't want to hurt their feelings, so you tell the classmate that you are busy that day. They ask you out again. You make up another excuse. However, sometimes people become more aggressive when they have not been firmly told no. When that happens, they might start sending you too many messages or even messages that refer to sex. They might even start showing up everywhere you are. That has moved from someone innocently asking you out and has crossed the line into sexual harassment.

As you get older and perhaps date more, you may find yourself in awkward, or uncomfortable, situations. This is part of dating—and life in general—and it simply cannot be avoided. The best way to avoid getting yourself into awkward situations is by being honest and up-front with people. In the short term, it might be easier to make up an excuse for why you cannot go out with someone. But it would have been better to respond to the request for a date with honesty and clarity. Hopefully, the person will appreciate your tact and stop asking you out.

If you don't return someone's interest, try saying, "I am flattered that you are interested in me, but I don't have the same feelings for you. Sorry."

One final note on flirting: flirting is a part of life. It is also fun and exciting—it is nice to have someone pay attention to you and want to engage in witty conversation. While it is easy to get caught up in the moment and flirt, always keep this in mind: flirting between adults and teenagers is never OK. It is inappropriate, and the adult is always at fault. An adult should know better. Always tell someone if an adult has stopped acting friendly and has started to flirt with you. And remember, you did not do anything wrong.

WHERE SEXUAL HARASSMENT OCCURS

Sadly, there is no safe space that can be guaranteed to be free from sexual harassment. There are certain places where it is more likely to occur, however, and equipping yourself with this knowledge can help you recognize and then act appropriately upon incidents of sexual harassment. The following sections outline some of the places where sexual harassment most often occurs.

SCHOOL

You spend more time at school than anywhere else. It is also a place that cannot be 100 percent supervised because the students greatly outnumber faculty and staff. According to the 2017–2018 Civil Rights Data Collection by the U.S. Department of Education, nearly 45,000 public school students reported being harassed or bullied on the basis of sex. A 2014 survey of middle school students found that the most likely places where students experienced harassment were hallways (22.7 percent) or classrooms (21.4 percent), with 13 percent occurring inside school gyms and 9.7 percent taking place near lockers. The most common form of sexual harassment reported was unwanted physical touching, at 21.6 percent.

RELIGIOUS SPACES

This may seem counterintuitive. Religious spaces are the places where people go for spirituality and to be closer to a higher power. However, these are also spaces where people place a great deal of trust in others and become vulnerable. Beyond physical touching and verbal abuse, some places of worship have reported church workers watching and showing pornography to their victims.

ON THE STREET

Statistics vary, but catcalling is one of the most common forms of sexual harassment. Both men and women may be victims of catcalling, but like most victims of harassment in general, women greatly outnumber men.

Many women are subjected to street harassment in public places. Examples include unwanted comments, gestures, and touching, generally from strangers.

AT WORK

More and more teenagers are working than ever before, and over summer break, of course, the number of teenage employees swells. Sadly, the workplace is one of the most common places for the sexual harassment of teens to occur. Major corporations and employers of teens, including Burger King, McDonald's, and Starbucks, have had to pay money to victims of sexual harassment. Managers and coworkers alike have harassed people at work and have even gone so far as to send unwelcome and explicit text messages.

ONLINE AND OVER THE PHONE

Between social media and apps like Kik, TikTok, Snapchat, Instagram, Twitter, and Tumblr—just to name a few—teenagers today find it harder to leave their school day behind than any generation before them. On any of these platforms, and inside any of these apps, sexual harassment can occur. Sending unsolicited texts and nudes are extremely common practices. So is sharing, without permission, nude photos that someone may have sent to another person, such as a partner, in the past. Additionally, many teenagers have experienced having their sex lives used against them, which is often known as slut shaming.

Sexual harassment is never acceptable in any of these settings. In every case, there are laws and policies in place intended to protect against harassment. Before the 1960s, discrimination against women was widely accepted, including sexual harassment by men in positions of greater power. Today, people recognize that the behavior is hurtful and demeaning, and there's no excuse for it.

Some sexual predators, knowing the types of workplaces that hire teenagers during the summer, frequent these establishments seeking targets for harassment.

CHAPTER 2

VICTIMS OF SEXUAL HARASSMENT

Sexual harassment is a painful and humiliating experience. Being a victim of sexual harassment can cause long-term consequences, from psychological scarring to the effects the harassment has on your everyday life. Remember that there are resources you can draw on to deal with the situation. If you're sexually harassed, you may find yourself denying or minimizing the experience and downplaying the emotional pain it caused. Try to accept what has happened and deal with your turbulent feelings rather than bottling up your hurt. Talk to family, friends, and a therapist, if you need help processing the experience.

On a practical level, keep a log of incidents of sexual harassment and save any records such as texts or pictures that demonstrate what happened. Be specific about times, locations, details of the interactions, and any other people present. Schools and workplaces have policies prohibiting sexual harassment, and there are laws that address inappropriate conduct in public places. If you can present detailed information demonstrating sexual harassment to the authorities, you'll be in a better position to have the situation resolved quickly and conclusively.

WHO CAN BE A VICTIM?

Anyone can be the victim of sexual harassment. A 2019 survey by the UC San Diego Center on Gender Equity and Health of adults across the country found that 81 percent of women and 43 percent of men had been sexually harassed and/or assaulted. Forty percent of women and 21 percent of men had been sexually harassed online. Twenty-seven percent of women and 11 percent of men were followed by a harasser. Of the victims, 18 percent of women and 16 percent of men reported that they had been sexually harassed within the past six months. The incidence was higher for lesbian and bisexual women than for any other group—39 percent reported that they had been sexually harassed in the last six months. Twenty-three percent of women and 12 percent of men changed their everyday routines or routes as a result of sexual harassment.

Youth are at risk of sexual harassment as well. According to the National Sexual Violence Resource Center, 56 percent of girls and 40 percent of boys between grades 7 and 12 had been sexually harassed. Fifty-two percent of girls and 35 percent of boys had been sexually harassed in person, while 36 percent of girls and 24 percent of boys had been sexually harassed online. LGBTQ+ youth were at a much higher risk, with 81 percent experiencing sexual harassment.

As seen, young women are more likely to be sexually harassed or abused than their male counterparts. This can manifest itself in pressure for dates and/or sex. Being pressured into sex is a big warning sign that you are not in a good relationship.

It's a red flag if a partner tries to pressure you into intimate activities as a test to prove your love. This demonstrates a lack of consideration for your boundaries.

Straight young men, too, can be victims of sexual harassment but make up a statistically smaller sample of victims. This is not to say that young men are not harassed more than reported. There is evidence that social pressure makes straight men of any age even more timid in reporting harassment than any other group. The numbers of harassment climb sharply for young men who identify as gay.

There is also one group not immediately thought of who can be damaged by sexual harassment: those who witness it. Evidence shows that those who routinely witness sexual harassment—most often occurring in schools—might begin to think of sexual harassment as normal. This can create a culture in which sexual harassment is thought to be "part of growing up." This is wrong.

One final note: sexual harassment isn't limited to any particular body type. A 15-year-old named Lindsay told Richa Gulati from *Teen Vogue* that when she was in seventh grade, "I was flat-chested when other girls started to develop, and I was told that I wasn't a girl," she says. It was not just her male classmates who were mean to her. She explains, "As I was getting ready for a school dance, girls came up to me to ask how I could hold up my dress when I didn't have breasts . . . They brought insecurity about my body to the surface."

Sexual harassment can damage the victim's self-esteem and lead to social withdrawal—avoiding opportunities to interact with friends, family, and peers.

HOW TO RESPOND

Sexual harassment can occur just about anywhere. A group of female students recently told the *Christian Science Monitor* that, even though they went to a so-called "good" school, they still experienced sexual harassment as freshmen: "Ten or so senior boys would line up at the stair balcony during class change—calling girls' names, trying to look down their shirts, and even spitting on some girls—which was disgusting." The solution was to avoid taking that stairway to class, but was that the best option?

Some schools are responsive to the issue of teenage sexual harassment, while others, sadly, will sometimes write off sexual harassment as "boys being boys."

If you are a victim of sexual harassment, you may feel scared, and you may feel like it is you against the world. But there are some immediate, practical steps you can take to help you battle back against this treatment. Remember that each situation is different, however, and there is no one right way when it comes to handling sexual harassment. That being said, the following list of tips should assist you

- Tell the harasser to stop. This may seem extremely obvious, but it is surprisingly rare that the person who is being harassed tells the harasser to stop. You can do this any of several ways: in person, over text, in an email, or in a letter. If you do write to your harasser, save a copy (save a copy of what you send no matter what means of communication you use). You may need it as evidence later if your harasser does not stop and you opt to report him or her.

- Tell a trusted adult. Perhaps you have a favorite teacher or a parent or other relative whom you trust with this kind of information. More and more schools have a staff member who is a dedicated counselor dealing with bullying (and remember, sexual harassment is a form of bullying). Most schools have systems set up to deal with this type of behavior.

- Keep a journal. This is extremely important. If your harasser sends you direct messages, whether they are offensive pictures, videos, or texts, save them all. Sexual harassment cases can come down to "he said, she said." Having evidence that you have been sexually harassed can prove to be vital, especially if legal action must be taken. Write down what happened, who was there (including people who did not harass you), how it made you feel, and what you did. Although it may be painful to recall the events, writing them down can also be a relief. Some victims have described writing as a way to help get the bad events out of their heads.

- Do not quit! If the first person you tell does not take you seriously, find another person. If he or she doesn't believe you, tell another person. The adults in your life have a responsibility to protect you from sexual harassment. If they are not taking that responsibility seriously, keep speaking out until you find someone who does.

Journals and other forms of documentation can serve as evidence demonstrating sexual harassment if you go to the authorities. Include as many specific details as possible.

AN UNDERREPORTED PROBLEM

As mentioned previously, the statistics about the frequency of incidents of sexual harassment are never as definite as we would like. Why is sexual harassment underreported in person and online? A 2014 study that took place in Belgium looked to find out by focusing on the online reporting of sexual harassment. Do any of their results sound familiar to you?

- Out of 300 teens who said they had been sexually harassed online, only 60 (or 20 percent) of students reported the abuse to a social media platform. Only about half received a response, and the content was removed in only 18 cases. The lack of response to each individual case and the incredibly few actions taken may make you think that nothing will be done, so you may as well not report it to begin with. This is not true. Remember, no one has the right to make you feel harassed, especially when you are trying to enjoy yourself online. If at first you don't get the help you need, keep looking until you do.

- Many students reported that they were concerned that complaining would not yield any results or could even make matters worse. Given the response rates, this idea is not without reality. However, ignoring harassment will not make it go away. This is a situation in which someone is trying to force you to react in a sexual way. Nothing is more personal, and few things are worse than trying to make someone physically afraid.

- Many of those surveyed did not do anything because they thought they were not harassed enough or the harassment was not "severe enough" to call for a report. This is also very dangerous. There is never a time when someone saying something sexual to you is OK if you did not invite them to do it. Do not think you have to cope with someone sexually harassing you because it was in the form of a joke as opposed to a deliberately provocative statement.

Sexual harassment is dramatically underreported in the workplace, as well. Often, the victims fear retaliation by their employer or expect inaction regarding their claim. Statistics demonstrate that this is a valid concern. According to *The Conversation*, about two-thirds of victims who file a complaint lose their jobs as a result. Only about a quarter receive any compensation, usually a monetary settlement, and employers agree to change workplaces in just 12 percent of cases. In a 2016 report on workplace sexual harassment, the EEOC recommended that company leadership make a commitment toward promoting a workplace culture that does not tolerate sexual harassment.

Workers who have been sexually harassed at work have options such as reporting it to their boss or filing a complaint with a government agency such as the EEOC.

MYTHS & FACTS

MYTH: Sexual harassment is often exaggerated, and most so-called harassment is harmless flirtation.

FACT: Most harassment has nothing to do with flirtation or true, sincere social or sexual interest. Like bullying, harassment is designed to intimidate and frighten. It can also be insulting or simply offensive to hear someone speak about your body that way. Many victims of sexual harassment rearrange their lives to avoid harassment. For example, they take different pathways to get to class, delete online profiles, or change their phone numbers.

MYTH: Only women can be victims of sexual harassment. Only men can be sexual harassers.

FACT: Although the majority of victims of sexual harassment are women, anyone can be harassed. Men may be harassed less as a whole, but the percentage of the population of victims of sexual harassment is much higher for gay men than heterosexual men. Also, there is a strong likelihood that people in every group, no matter how they identify, underreport sexual harassment. Transgender youth in particular experience extremely high rates of sexual abuse and assault.

MYTH: Victims of sexual harassment generally provoke harassment by the way they behave, how they dress, or how they look.

FACT: While it is slowly beginning to be challenged in society at large, there are still many people who will blame victims for the inappropriate behavior of their harassers. This is referred to as "victim blaming," as well as "asking for it." No one asks to be spoken to or touched simply because of their clothing choices or makeup, or because they had a fun time at a party.

There are many myths about sexual harassment that tend to minimize the seriousness of the issue or blame the victim rather than the offender.

CHAPTER 3

SEEKING HELP

The experience of sexual harassment can leave a victim feeling a variety of strong emotions—shame, anger, helplessness, sadness, fear, hopelessness. Victims can be overwhelmed with self-doubt afterward. Each person responds in a different way to the experience, and there may be long-term aftereffects. A victim may feel anxious or depressed, especially if they already had a tendency toward these conditions, and the emotional issues can be accompanied by physical symptoms such as headaches or general muscle aches. This is because the parts of the brain that manage emotional stress also affect physical functions.

A victim of sexual harassment may have trouble with performance at work or school. The people around them can even be adversely affected, too—it's not easy to see a colleague or peer subjected to harassment. Remember that sexual harassment is not your fault, and you're not alone. There are people who have survived similar experiences and people who want to help you heal. Some victims even find that reaching out to help others—through a support group, advocacy, or volunteering, for example—can work to bring closure to their own painful experience.

Sexual harassment can cause long-term effects for victims. Just because the event is over it does not necessarily mean a victim has been able to move past the experience. Here are some of the most common long-term effects.

A sexual harassment support group is made up of people who have all shared the experience of being sexually harassed. They share personal stories and coping strategies with each other.

DEPRESSION AND ANXIETY

Depression is the most common effect of sexual harassment. This is a serious problem and is probably best addressed with a therapist or counselor. A long-term study found that of 1,000 youths who had been sexually harassed in their teens and early 20s, most still show symptoms of depression in their 30s. Victims can also experience anxiety and panic attacks following incidents of sexual harassment.

A victim of sexual harassment may experience mental and physical effects long after it has happened. A counselor or therapist can help you move past the incident.

PTSD

Post-traumatic stress disorder (PTSD) has also been found in numerous studies of sexual harassment victims. One sign that you may be experiencing PTSD is avoiding the people and places that remind you of when you were harassed. Another is reexperiencing the event or experiencing frequent recall of upsetting, disturbing memories of what happened.

Never underestimate just how damaging sexual harassment can be. Consider this: according to a Livescience article by Rachael Rettner, women in the military who have been sexually harassed develop PTSD at a rate of four times that of women who go to combat. To put it another way, many women in the military find combat easier to deal with than sexual harassment.

Post-traumatic stress disorder (PTSD) can be caused by many types of traumatic events, such as combat exposure, physical assault, abuse, or sexual harassment.

THOUGHTS OF SUICIDE

One of the most dangerous effects of sexual harassment is suicidal thoughts. According to the Rachael Rettner article, in a study of 1,000 Canadian high school students, 23 percent said they had experienced some form of sexual harassment in the last six months. Of that group, 15 percent said they had made suicide attempts or had thought about suicide, compared to just 2 percent of students who hadn't experienced sexual harassment.

If you have suicidal thoughts, seek help immediately.

SLEEP PROBLEMS AND SUBSTANCE ABUSE

Two other common long-term effects of sexual harassment are two sides of the same coin: sleep problems and substance abuse. In the case of sleep problems, the increased levels of stress and anxiety can create restlessness. Some victims report an inability to sleep at night. They lie awake reliving the events in their heads, which thwarts their ability to relax. Still others have reported that they have such terrible nightmares about when they were harassed that they would prefer not to sleep.

An inability to escape the horrible memories is also one of the major reasons victims turn to alcohol or drugs. Often, people make the mistake of thinking that, for example, someone got really drunk and then something bad happened. But it is just as likely, if not more so, that someone got extremely drunk because something bad happened to him or her. Studies have shown that, for example, women in college who drink heavily are more likely to have been victims of sexual harassment (or worse) when they were younger.

A victim of sexual harassment may have trouble sleeping, returning to everyday routines, and enjoying favorite activities. Turning to drugs or alcohol won't help.

YOUR EMOTIONAL SUPPORT SYSTEM

Many people do not know how to help victims of sexual harassment. Because the damage from sexual harassment is not physical, it can be difficult for people to understand that you are not yourself. They may tell you to move on with your life and to accept what happened.

So, what can you do? The following is a list containing some options for finding emotional support:

- Talk to people about what happened. You will be pleasantly surprised that for every person who tells you to move on, there will be even more people who want to listen to your story. It is important to talk about what happened to you. It may be therapeutic for you to express your feelings. And talking about your experience may help others; other victims may realize that they are not alone, simply because you shared what happened to you.

- Do not let others tell you "what really happened." Nor should you let people tell you how you should deal with being a victim of sexual harassment. We are all different and each situation is unique. There is no one-size-fits-all solution for something as complex as sexual harassment.

- Join a support group. There is a good chance that there is a support group near you where people gather together, listen to one another, and help each other heal. Online support groups can also help you work through your thoughts and feelings. Studies of support groups show that people are more likely to accomplish their goals (in this case, recovering from sexual harassment) in a group than by themselves.

- Write about your experience. The power of writing has historically been a great way to express yourself. A journal may be a way to articulate your feelings in a private way. You never have to show anyone your words, unless you want to.

Journaling can significantly benefit mental health. Writing down thoughts and feelings can help people process them and put them into perspective.

- Get beyond shame or self-blaming. This is easier said than done and can take a long time for some victims of sexual harassment. When something bad happens to you, it is tempting to think you did something wrong. You didn't. The person who harassed you is the one in the wrong.

- Try to grow your social circle in a positive way. Perhaps when you were being harassed, a friend didn't believe you. It may be time to find a new friend to confide in. A true friend will believe you and support you, especially when it comes to something as important as your emotional well-being and physical safety.

Difficult situations such as sexual harassment can test friendships. Surround yourself with friends who support you and have your best interests in mind.

- Therapy or counseling may be an option. Find a place that has access to a therapist who understands what victims who have been sexually harassed are experiencing. Only now is the therapist community beginning to understand the long-term effects that sexual harassment can have on teens. If you cannot find someone trained or experienced in this area, a sexual assault or abuse counselor may be a good place to start.

TAKING LEGAL ACTION

Some victims of sexual harassment decide that they wish to take their harasser to court. For some, seeing their case through the justice system gives them satisfaction and closure.

Maybe you are a victim of sexual harassment at school, and you have told someone and nothing is happening. Or perhaps you told someone and the pain is too great. Whatever your circumstances, you may decide to go to court. What happens next depends greatly on whether or not the person who harassed you is an adult or fellow teenager.

When an adult who works for the school harasses you, generally the school district is sued. The idea is that the adult is a representative of the school district and therefore the school district is responsible. The drawback with this strategy is that unless supervisors at the district level knew about it and there is hard evidence, a verdict in your favor will depend greatly upon many circumstances beyond your control. It is also common for the victim to sue the school official who harassed them. Again, evidence plays a key role—so keep that journal and all the messages and gather witnesses.

If another student is harassing you, things can get very complex very quickly. An article by Alexandra Yoon-Hendricks for the *Daily Californian* offers one example. In 2016, a 16-year-old Berkeley High School student sued the school district for not properly handling her case. The lawsuit said that she had been persistently stalked and harassed by a male student. The victim filled out a statement and spoke with the vice principal, but the vice principal failed to notify the director of student services and the on-campus police officer, which was against district policy. The day after, the victim and her mother met with the vice principal and a police official. The police official did not act properly, allegedly asking the victim, "Why didn't you report him earlier?" and suggesting that the student invited the predatory behavior.

Shocked, the victim asked that the harasser be arrested and charged, to which the police official said, "We are trying to keep these young men out of the system."

A few days later, the victim was harassed again. She was so upset that she didn't attend school for more than a month. When she finally returned to school, specific routes to class were given to both the harassed student and the harassing student. The victim was also promised an escort to class, but the school never came through with one.

The student from Berkeley High School did everything right. She reported the incident to school officials, for example, and she told her mother. But the system designed to protect her failed. So she decided to hire a lawyer and take her case to court.

Although plenty of sexual harassment occurs online, the law has not currently adjusted quickly enough to cover these types of situations. But your actions should still be the same, no matter how or where you were sexually harassed. Document the incidents, report the incidents, do not give up until you are satisfied with the outcome, and take care of yourself. If you experience physical and emotional health consequences, take them seriously. There are counselors who specialize in treating people who have been sexually harassed or abused. If you're tempted to isolate yourself with your feelings of pain or shame, reach out to your friends and family. A single harasser may have caused you great harm, but you're surrounded by people who want to see you heal and thrive.

If a student makes a sexual harassment complaint, the school is required to investigate it and provide the student with protection if necessary.

10 GREAT QUESTIONS TO ASK A CAMPUS SAFETY OFFICIAL

1. Where can I find the school's policy on sexual harassment?

2. Does the school admit there is a problem with sexual harassment?

3. What are the punishments for people who sexually harass other students? Expulsion? Suspension? Is it left to law enforcement?

4. Can students report harassment anonymously?

5. Does the school enforce no-contact orders?

6. What is the policy for missing class as a result of being a victim of sexual harassment?

7. Does the school have or allow student organizations to educate people about and stop sexual violence?

8. Are there any staff members or counselors who are trained to deal specifically with teenage sexual harassment?

9. If sexual harassment has occurred, does the school have services on the school grounds for helping victims?

10. What additional resources are available in the community for victims of sexual harassment?

Most schools have resources for victims of sexual harassment, such as security measures, counseling support, and advocates who can offer assistance.

CHAPTER 4

ONLINE SEXUAL HARASSMENT

According to a 2019 report by Common Sense Media, teenagers spend an average of 9 hours in front of screens every day. It might seem that online activities would be safe from the worst aspects of sexual harassment, such as touching or physical intimidation. But sexual harassment has followed kids online, and technology has even enabled new ways of harassing victims. Today, an online stalker or harasser can often learn a great deal of personal information about their target that would have been difficult to find without the internet. Harassers can hide behind anonymity when they post or send harassing content. Many people are willing to make hurtful comments online that they would never dare to say face-to-face.

Online sexual harassment is highly prevalent on the internet, and it's a growing problem. According to a 2021 survey by Pew, 11 percent of adults reported being sexually harassed online, and 11 percent had been stalked. In 2015, that figure was just 5 percent and 7 percent, respectively. Younger people were more likely to report being sexually harassed online. Of 18- to 30-year-olds, 25 percent had been sexually harassed online, and 21 percent had been stalked. Women were also likelier to report online sexual harassment—16 percent of all adults—or being stalked—13 percent. Two-thirds of respondents who had been sexually harassed online believed that it was because of their gender.

Americans report experiencing more severe forms of online harassment, including sexual harassment and stalking, since 2014. Social media is the most common space where harassment occurs.

INFORMATION OVERLOAD

People often don't give much thought to the amount of personal and even private information that they share online. If you post a message on social media about your plans for the evening, you're probably thinking that your audience is made up of friends and peers. But harassers can use the internet to learn about your lifestyle and daily habits. Here are some examples of information that teenagers commonly share online.

Photos of themselves: Selfies are the most common items posted on social media by teens. Teens need to be careful of their privacy settings. Harassers can use these photos. And be especially careful if your friends list or your followers contain strangers.

Their school's name: By posting your school's name, you advertise certain telling facts, such as you are a teenager and also where you will be for six or seven hours a day Monday through Friday.

Their relationship status: If you are single, harassers may look at this as an invitation to get you into a conversation and push to take it to a sexual level. If you are in a relationship, some people may try to pry into your intimate life.

Videos of themselves: The content of videos can vary widely

and so will the attention they bring. For example, predators might not be very interested in seeing your school band recital, but a public video of you dancing in your room could bring unwanted attention. Be aware of your privacy settings.

Remember, once something is on the internet, it's there forever. You can never completely erase it. Be smart about what you post and pay attention to who will see it.

A harasser can use the internet to learn about a victim's habits and locations. Guard against online stalkers by keeping personal information private.

BLOCKING OUT THE HARASSMENT

Today's teens often wish they did not have to have social media. Some of them even think it is ruining their lives, but if they did not have it, then they would feel isolated. One such person is Christina, who lives in Austin, Texas. Only 15 years old, she repeatedly negotiated advances made by an older boy. He followed her around across multiple social networks. Additionally, whenever Christina posted selfies, her teenage harasser would screenshot them and post them to Snapchat. She figured he had quite the collection.

Then the stalking and harassing behavior switched from online to real life. He sent her a message that he was going to her house. Christina replied that he shouldn't go there, and her family wasn't even home. But he didn't listen to her request and went to her house anyway. However, she did not feel that this was enough to make her want to talk to an adult or counselor. Instead, she blocked him and made another account.

While it is tempting to block someone and/or create a new account, there is a problem with this. Namely, teenage girls begin to think that the behavior of their harassers is normal and a problem for them to handle on their own. Unfortunately, this approach ignores the bigger problem of males thinking that they have a right to a female's time, attention, physical space, or body. To think of it another way, while blocking someone potentially creates a safe space for you, it does not change the actions of the person harassing you. For this type of behavior to change, the person has to be reported.

Always report this behavior to a parent or trusted adult, even if the actions or comments seem like they are no big deal. If it makes you the least bit uncomfortable, tell an adult.

Social media keeps users connected with others, but it can also enable harmful interactions and leave users feeling anxious and isolated.

GAMERGATE

In 2014, a misogynistic harassment campaign called Gamergate roiled the internet. It began with a single blog post by Eron Gjoni, in which he claimed that his ex-girlfriend, video game developer Zoë Quinn, had cheated on him. Additionally, he said that people in the video game industry and the media traded sex with her for development opportunities and positive press coverage. Even though these events were proven to be false, and the blog post alone is sexual harassment, a controversy about her raged online.

What was one man's grudge against his ex-girlfriend quickly grew as people with connections to sites like 4chan began to attack female journalist Anita Sarkeesian, a self-described feminist writer. Shortly after that, journalist Jenn Frank and game designer Mattie Brice both quit their jobs because of harassment. Additionally, games developer Brianna Wu came under attack.

All the women mentioned received numerous death threats, threats to their families, and some were even told they would be raped—all over social media, Twitter in particular. Both Quinn and Wu had their phone numbers and addresses made public. The threats were so extreme that they left their houses.

The Gamergate episode foreshadowed a societal shift toward deep ideological divisions marked by extremist views and behavior, conspiracy theories, and targeted harassment. The tactics used during Gamergate have come to serve as a template for toxic and threatening harassment campaigns.

In 2015, Zoë Quinn and Anita Sarkeesian spoke before the United Nations about their experiences during a panel discussion about gendered sexual harassment online.

PROTECTING YOUR PRIVACY

Between your smartphone, computer, and tablet, there are many places where your information and media (pictures, texts, etc.) can easily be stolen. This may make them easy targets for harassers. There are some basic steps you can take to make your social media accounts less tempting for potential harassers.

- Manage your privacy settings: This is the most basic thing you can do to help protect yourself. Nearly every social media outlet allows you to control your privacy settings. It is in your best interest to set everything to private or friends only. On Instagram, for example, it is easy to set your account to private. This allows you to approve everyone who follows you and prevents your photos from being public. While everyone wants to have more followers, be smart about it.

- Do not become "friends" with people you do not know: Check to see if you have mutual friends. If you do, ask them about the person. If you do not have any mutual friends, ignore their request.

- Never respond to inappropriate requests, report them: Many teens, especially teenage girls, receive inappropriate messages online. If someone you do not know starts asking questions about your personal life, ask yourself, "Why are they asking me this and what can they do with this information?" The last thing you want to do is to provide a would-be predator with volunteered information. Do not reply to these messages.

- Avoid posting or sending inappropriate or sexual pictures and comments. Expressing your sexuality is something you have the right to do, but it is best done in private. If you post it on social media, even if your account is set to private, it can be hacked, forwarded to other people, or copied.

Change your social media settings to private in order to prevent strangers from coming across your account—they might not have friendly intentions.

When it comes to how to protect your account passwords and devices, Karen S., who has worked in New York City's bustling tech start-up scene for more than eight years and has led workshops on protecting yourself online, has some tips. "At every tech company I've worked for, we took security very seriously," she says. "We encrypt messages and use password managers. While there aren't millions of dollars at stake for personal users, the general public, and teenagers especially, should take steps to protect their devices and their accounts."

She offered the following six tips to help prevent harassers from stealing your identity or information and then using it against you:

1. Create a unique password for each account and each device. While this may sound like a lot of work, you can use a free password manager like LastPass.
2. Create a better password. When it comes to passwords, you never want to make them anything obvious. Instead, you should create a longer password, something at least 15 characters long.
3. Lock your device every time you walk away from it. This is especially important, say, in a school, which is where most teen harassment begins.
4. Be selective about which wireless networks you join. Make sure it is a network that you know. Also, do not always have Wi-Fi enabled on your phone, otherwise you might join a network that is bad and not even know it!
5. Turn off location settings on your device. Karen tells people, "Whether it is for photos, or anything

else, turn your location setting off. Some apps may say they can't work when location is disabled, but often if you hit ignore, the app will work just fine." Remember, one way harassers may harass you is by showing up where you are. Not only can this cause mental discomfort, but it can also put you in physical danger.

6. Set up a remote wiping system. This advanced step essentially allows you to reset your phone from a different device if someone should ever steal it.

Online sexual harassment can lead to feelings of stress and trauma. Seek help if you have mental or physical health symptoms from your experiences of online sexual harassment. Consider spending more time at online communities with policies that explicitly respect your privacy and allow you to set your own boundaries.

Turn off your location setting when taking photos and using apps. This will protect your device as well as your own privacy.

CHAPTER 5

BEING AN ALLY

Sexual harassment can derail victims' lives and create a toxic work or learning environment. High-profile cases of sexual harassment or assault regularly appear in headlines, serving as a disquieting reminder of the continued prevalence of the problem. Even if you've never personally experienced sexual harassment, you might feel compelled to take action against it. Maybe you want to show support for your peers, or perhaps you want to take a stand for justice for all. There are ways that you can make a difference in your own school and play a small part in changing a society that too often minimizes instances of sexual harassment.

A program that has proven effective in empowering people to confront sexual harassment is called bystander intervention training. The approach is based on the assumption that the trainees in the program are allies who have an interest in addressing sexual harassment, not skeptics who have to be convinced that sexual harassment is a real problem. Onlookers tend to freeze when they observe instances of harassment because they don't know how they can help. Bystander intervention training teaches techniques such as direct involvement or distraction that can interrupt a sexual harassment incident. The strategies can also be used to intervene in other scenarios, such as bullying or racially motivated harassment.

Social media keeps users connected with others, but it can also enable harmful interactions and leave users feeling anxious and isolated.

BEING RESPECTFUL

In 2016, singer and actress Ariana Grande encountered a fan while she was out with her boyfriend. The man was incredibly excited to meet her, but his behavior could be considered harassment. He talked about how "Ariana is sexy as hell, man!" and then congratulated her boyfriend for having a sexual relationship with her. This way of talking about Grande made her an object and not a person.

Singer and actress Ariana Grande felt sickened by a fan's inappropriate comments that objectified her. On social media, she urged other women not to tolerate those types of comments.

As we have read throughout this resource, although anyone can be harassed—women, men, and people from all minority groups, including LGBTQ+—women of all ages are disproportionately targeted for sexual harassment. Perhaps, if you're a young man, reading about sexual harassment makes you wonder what you can do to help. Maybe as you read you want to come up with ways to help stop the culture of toxic masculinity that allows the sexual harassment of women to occur. Or perhaps you wonder what you could do if you, like Grande's boyfriend, heard another man speaking about a woman you care about, whether they are a partner, family member, friend, or acquaintance. Below are four tips designed just for you!

1. Listen to your female and minority friends. They are the ones who experience this, and they are the ones to tell you what happened. As you listen to their stories, you can learn to identify sexual harassment when it happens.
2. Ask, "Are you OK?" This might sound easier to do than it actually is. If your friend is being harassed right in front of you or you suspect that she is, ask her, "Are you OK?" If she answers no or you think she might be scared to say yes, stay with her, and, if you feel like it is safe to do so, stand between your friend and the person harassing. Again, sexual harassment is about power, and often the harasser might be afraid to continue if you are standing between your friend and the harasser. Be sure to keep both your friend and yourself safe from harm if at all possible.

3. After you know your friend is OK, tell the harasser to stop. It is important to note that you are not looking to get into a fight. Your goal is to get him to leave and for the situation to end peacefully.
4. Include more people. Because the type of sexual harassment we are talking about is occurring in real life, chances are that it will be in a public or community space. While you confront the harasser, speak with confidence and call on others to talk about what they see. They may be just as upset as you but unwilling to speak unless called upon. The more people there are saying that the sexual harassment is unacceptable, the less likely it is that the harasser will continue. And perhaps he will think twice about doing it again in the future.

Additionally, there are many men of all ages who are ignorant about sexual harassment. If they are willing to listen, share the facts about sexual harassment, whom it happens to, and the statistics. You might just make the world a better place!

If you observe sexual harassment occurring and you don't think it would be safe to confront a harasser, inform the authorities instead.

SHOWING SUPPORT

Chances are there is a girl at your school who tends to be harassed for her body shape or size, or a boy who's harassed because he doesn't fit in with the rest of the guys. Maybe another student is going through a gender transition. There are things you can do to make all of these people feel like they are not alone and that harassment is not OK.

Friendly support can make a big difference. Often times, victims of sexual harassment think they are alone. So, consider joining them during lunch, free time like study hall, or physical education class. The times at school when they are not in a classroom setting are often when your peers are most vulnerable, and then they become targets for harassers.

Follow the models in the examples for young men discussed previously. Say something to the person who is harassing your schoolmate. Of course, try to do it in a way that does not make the situation worse, but often simply telling someone what he is doing is wrong is enough to make the bully stop.

Finally, always tell an adult at school what is happening.

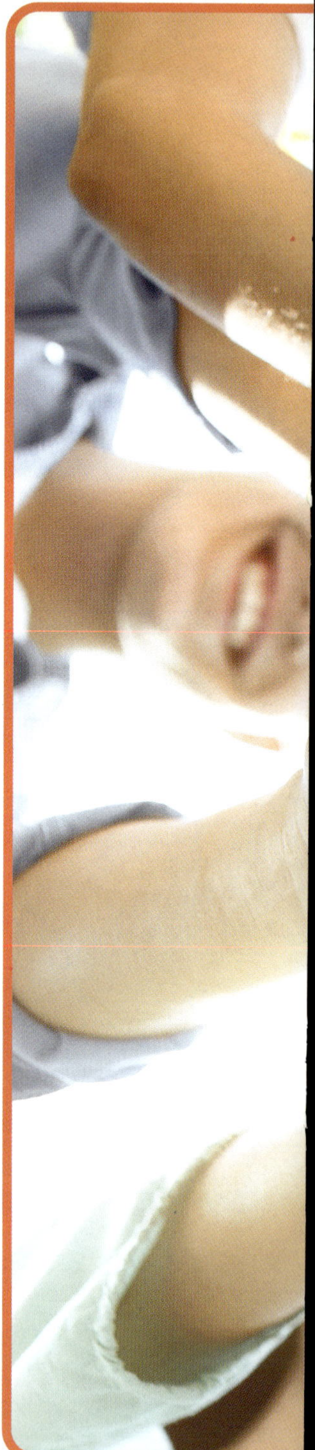

You can promote inclusiveness by learning more about other people's identities and trying to make people different from yourself feel welcome.

RAISING YOUR VOICE

In March 2016, a group of students at Tualatin High School in Oregon began posting anonymously on the web page Project Girls with Guts. They all had one thing in common: they did not feel that the school's administration was taking their claims of sexual harassment and assault seriously enough. A few students who had had these experiences started talking and then the circle grew as they found more and more students who had also experienced sexual harassment or even assault.

THE #METOO MOVEMENT

On October 15, 2017, actress Alyssa Milano addressed a tweet to her followers: "If you've been sexually harassed or assaulted write 'me too' as a reply to this tweet." She received a flood of replies and catalyzed a national dialog. Women from around the world, some of them well-known, told their stories of being harassed or assaulted.

Milano was motivated by revelations that the influential film producer Harvey Weinstein had sexually exploited numerous women over his decades long career. The movement that came to be known as #MeToo brought attention to an issue that had often been overlooked. Survivors of sexual violence sometimes felt marginalized or even stigmatized when they called for justice. The #MeToo movement gave a sense of solidarity and support to women who had been harassed or assaulted. It put a spotlight on the extent of the problem that many women face in their daily lives. And the movement brought real change.

After #MeToo, there were high-profile cases in which men faced serious consequences after accusations of sexual assault and harassment. States have enacted new sexual harassment laws protecting workers. Some states have also addressed how sex crimes are handled, from the processing of rape kits to changing the statute of limitations for reporting an assault.

The #MeToo movement has spotlighted high-profile instances of sexual harassment and raised awareness of the issue among young women across the world.

A young man (no names are used because they are all minors) was accused by two separate students of assault, and the response the students received from a counselor in a meeting was, "You have to remember that accusations are just accusations." It was clear that the school was not going to help them. The students were told that if they did not want to have any interaction with the student, they would have to avoid him. So, the students began to take action.

Angi Coleman was in a unique position to help. This former Tualatin student had moved to Florida, so she was able to assist her friends at Tualatin without worry about the school pressuring her or anyone getting upset—she lived across the country. She used her Twitter account to put out a call to her former classmates for their experiences with sexual harassment at the school. Within days, 24 students had replied, some of whom had not even told their parents what had happened to them.

Students in the school's Advocates for Gender Equality club have since combined forces with nearby Sherwood High School's Club Fem for an event called Speak Up—Raising Awareness of Sexual Assault.

This is a wonderful example of what you could do at your school or in your community. Students have traditionally organized in America to bring about change. Now, with more access to information and more communication channels, young people can work within their schools to demand change. As mentioned previously, sexual harassment comes out of bullying culture, and peer-to-peer work is often more effective than hoping school

Consider working to create a safe space in your school where students can talk about difficult experiences such as sexual harassment.

administrators can take care of things. Nevertheless, always be respectful and discuss solutions.

BEING A FRIEND

Often when someone has been sexually harassed, the first person they tell is a close friend. If a friend shares with you that they have been sexually harassed, you can support your friend as they begin to cope and heal. A friend may tell you right away or months later; either way your number-one responsibility is to listen.

As you have learned, the effect that sexual harassment has on victims can be life changing. They may experience anxiety, shock, anger, sadness, shame, or any combination of these feelings. They might even wonder if it is their fault. When listening to their story, try to keep these things in mind:

- Believe the victim. They have been through something horrible. Even if you have doubts, now is not the time to express them. Your friend has experienced a violation and they need to know that you are there for them.

- Put your emotions to the side. However, you are feeling—and anger is a perfectly appropriate response—the most important emotions are the victim's emotions. You will have time to process the events in time, but your complete attention should be given to the victim.

- Support your friend. Your friend is not at fault. No one hopes to be a victim of sexual harassment. Recall that your friend may be blaming himself or herself for what happened.

After your friend has told you what happened, do some research and find ways that you can help. But remember that everybody heals at their own pace and through their own process. Let them know that you're there for them, ready to listen to what they have to say without judging them.

Meanwhile, learn how you can work to end sexual harassment in your school and community. Let your school and city leaders know that you support laws and policies that provide clear recourses and protections for the victim. During times that sexual harassment becomes a matter of national discussion, let your policy makers know that you believe that sexual harassment should not be tolerated and that victims should be given a voice to call for change.

Sometimes the best thing you can do for a friend in pain is be a good listener. Be supportive and respect their decisions.

GLOSSARY

abuse To use improperly or treat in a harmful manner.

awkward Causing or involving embarrassment.

catcalling Saying or doing inappropriate things, such as whistling or commenting, to others when they are in public; often of a sexual nature.

consent To agree to something or give permission for something to occur.

counterintuitive Contrary to what seems to be true by instinct.

encrypt To put information into secret codes to prevent unapproved viewing.

harassment Persistent behavior that bothers, torments, or intimidates another person.

lewd Offensive in a sexual way.

manifest To demonstrate or show.

misogynistic Showing hatred of or prejudice against women.

overtone A hint toward something without actually saying what one means.

provocative Deliberately intended to elicit a reaction.

safe space A place where a person or group of people (for example, LGBTQ+ people) can feel confident they won't be exposed to emotional or physical harm.

sexual predator Someone who tries to have, or has had, sexual contact with another person in an abusive manner.

slut shaming Saying nasty things about someone for the sexual acts they have engaged in.

statistical Relating to statistics, which is the science of collecting and studying data.

traumatic Emotionally upsetting or shocking.

unsolicited Not asked for.

verdict A decision made by a court of law.

vital Absolutely crucial or necessary.

FOR MORE INFORMATION

GIRLS FOR GENDER EQUITY

25 Chapel Street, Suite 1006
Brooklyn, NY 11201
(718) 857-1393
Email: media@ggenyc.org
Website: www.ggenyc.org
Facebook: @GirlsForGenderEquity
Twitter: @GGENYC
Instagram: @ggenyc
Girls for Gender Equity works toward gender and racial justice from a Black feminist angle with youth-led programming and advocacy.

LEANIN.ORG

855 El Camino Real Suite 13A #262
Palo Alto, CA 94301
Email: info@leanin.org
Website: leanin.org
Facebook: @leanincommunity
Instagram, Twitter: @leaninorg
LeanIn.org works to help women achieve their professional ambitions and overcome barriers in the workplace. Resources for dealing with sexual harassment can be found at https://leanin.org/sexual-harassment.

MEN STOPPING VIOLENCE

2785 Lawrenceville Highway, Suite 112
Decatur, GA 30033
(404) 270-9894
Website: menstoppingviolence.org
Facebook: @MenStoppingViolence
Twitter: @MenStopViolence
Men Stopping Violence engages men and communities to put a stop to violence against women through education and by building a network of accountability.

METRAC

158 Spadina Road
Toronto, ON M5R 2T8
Canada
(416) 392-3135
Email: info@metrac.org
Website: www.metrac.org
Facebook: @METRACorg
Twitter: METRACorg
The mission of METRAC is to concentrate on education and prevention to change policies, ideas, and actions in order to halt violence against women and youth.

NATIONAL WOMEN'S LAW CENTER

11 Dupont Circle NW, Suite 800
Washington, DC 20036
(202) 588-5180
Website: nwlc.org
Facebook: @NWLC
Twitter: @NWLC
Instagram: @nationalwomenslawcenter
The National Women's Law Center advocates for the rights of girls and women in public policy, the courts, and society to find solutions to gender inequality and to help break down barriers.

RAPE, ABUSE & INCEST NATIONAL NETWORK (RAINN)

1220 L Street, NW Suite 505
Washington, D.C. 20005
(202) 544-1034
Website: rainn.org
Facebook: @RAINN01
Instagram, Twitter: @RAINN
RAINN is an anti–sexual violence organization that provides victim services, education, and public policy advocacy. Information and resources regarding sexual harassment are available at https://www.rainn.org/articles/sexual-harassment.

STOP SEXUAL ASSAULT IN SCHOOLS

4126 Circle Court SE
Lacey, WA 98503
Email: info@stopsexualassaultinschools.org
Website: stopsexualassaultinschools.org
Facebook: @StopSexualAssaultInHighSchool
Twitter: @SSAISorg
Instagram: @SSAISorg

The purpose of Stop Sexual Assault in Schools is to end gender discrimination, sexual harassment, and sexual assault for students from kindergarten through 12th grade. The group provides outreach services and educational resources to schools, groups, and individuals.

FOR FURTHER READING

Brezina, Corona. *Helping a Friend Who Is Being Bullied*. New York, NY: Rosen Publishing, 2017.

Freitas, Donna. *The Big Questions Book of Sex and Consent*. Montclair, NJ: Levine Querido, 2020.

Gitlin, Martin. *Helping a Friend in an Abusive Relationship*. New York, NY: Rosen Publishing, 2017.

Gurtler, Janet. *You Too?* Toronto, ON: Inkyard Press, 2020.

Hamilton, Tracy Brown. *Combating Internet Shaming*. New York, NY: Rosen Publishing, 2017.

Klein, Rebecca T. *Transgender Rights and Protections*. New York, NY: Rosen Publishing, 2017.

Leavitt, Amie. *Combating Toxic Online Communities*. New York, NY: Rosen Publishing, 2017.

Meyer, Susan. *Combatting "Slut" Shaming*. New York, NY: Rosen Publishing, 2017.

New York Times Editorial Staff. *#MeToo: Women Speak Out Against Sexual Assault*. New York, NY: New York Times Educational Publishing in association with The Rosen Publishing Group, Inc., 2019.

Orr, Tamra B. *I Have Been Shamed on the Internet. Now What?* New York, NY: Rosen Publishing, 2017.

INDEX

P

Q

R

S

ABOUT THE AUTHOR

ROSE MCCARTHY is an author who has written numerous books for children and young adults. Several have addressed social and legal issues faced by teens. She lives in New York.

PHOTO CREDITS

Cover, Photographee.eu/Shutterstock.com; Cover, pp. 1, 3-80 STUDIO DREAM/Shutterstock.com; Cover, p. 1 HIGOOD/Shutterstock.com; p. 5 Vereshchagin Dmitry/Shutterstock.com; p. 7 ibreakstock/Shutterstock.com; p. 8 Mangostar/Shutterstock.com; p. 9 https://commons.wikimedia.org/wiki/File:Anita_Hill_(40110509291).jpg; p. 11 tommaso79/Shutterstock.com; p. 13 MDV Edwards/Shutterstock.com; pp. 15, 65 Monkey Business Images/Shutterstock.com; p. 18 SpeedKingz/Shutterstock.com; p. 19 Daisy Daisy/Shutterstock.com; p. 20 DGLimages/Shutterstock.com; p. 22 Kosim Shukurov/Shutterstock.com; p. 25 kittirat roekburi/Shutterstock.com; p. 27 Radoslaw Korga/Shutterstock.com; p. 29 SeventyFour/Shutterstock.com; p. 30 Pixel-Shot/Shutterstock.com; pp. 31, 41 LightField Studios/Shutterstock.com; p. 33 Roman Chazov/Shutterstock.com; p. 35 Hrytsiv Oleksandr/Shutterstock.com; p. 36 mavo/Shutterstock.com; p. 39 Roman Samborskyi/Shutterstock.com; p. 43 tairome/Shutterstock.com; p. 45 chainarong06/Shutterstock.com; p. 47 Ermolaev Alexander/Shutterstock.com; p. 49 https://commons.wikimedia.org/wiki/File:Anita_Sarkeesian_2013.jpg; p. 51 mimagephotography/Shutterstock.com; p. 53 Mirage_studio/Shutterstock.com; p. 55 Dragon Images/Shutterstock.com; p. 56 Sky Cinema/Shutterstock.com; p. 59 Rido/Shutterstock.com; p. 61 Prostock-studio/Shutterstock.com; p. 63 Sundry Photography/Shutterstock.com; p. 67 Martin Novak/Shutterstock.com.